SECOND BEST MOMENTS
IN CHINESE HISTORY

THE UNIVERSITY OF
W   CHESTER

D1420297

Also by Frank Kuppner from Carcanet

Everything is Strange

FRANK KUPPNER

SECOND BEST MOMENTS
IN CHINESE HISTORY

CARCANET

First published in 1997 by
Carcanet Press Limited
4th Floor, Conavon Court
12–16 Blackfriars Street
Manchester M3 5BQ

A CIP catalogue record for this book
is available from the British Library
ISBN 1 85754 310 6

The publisher acknowledges financial assistance
from the Arts Council of England

Funded by
THE
ARTS
COUNCIL
OF ENGLAND

Set in Ehrhardt by Ensystems, Saffron Walden
Printed and bound in England by SRP Ltd, Exeter

Contents

To my good friend, RFB

Book One

A Moral Victory for the Barbarians

1

A slight rustle of leaves on a commonplace summer's day.
Two hours. Three hours. Four hours. Five hours.
A rustle of leaves on a nondescript summer's evening.
The poet suddenly rises and starts his journey home.

2

An old man is visible in the open doorway.
The traveller glances into the open doorway,
Then continues his journey through the mist-filled mountains.
The old man walks across and shuts the door.

3

The clouds are dark and close above the pleasure-garden.
It seems an inappropriate day for happiness.
A day when laughter on an upper balcony
Must have dropped down from the other side of the sky.

4

The bureaucrat sighs as he adds up another column.
Who can possibly be riding so many horses?
He sighs again, and glances down from his low pavilion.
A royal dog is staring at him insolently.

5

Observe the casements behind which lamps are shining.
It looks as if the whole city is preoccupied
On this gloomy, nondescript autumnal evening.
Why is a confused humanity wasting so much light?

6

The man slumped, dreaming, in the small pavilion
Is the same man as the one climbing the mountain path towards him.
In a minute or so, he shall pass by very close,
Although not quite close enough for recognition.

7

The scholars have gathered in a clearing in the wood.
Nervously at first, but with ever-growing enthusiasm,
They begin to discuss the insoluble problems of existence.
Soon, the forest resounds to their obscene drinking songs.

8

It is said that the great poet often used to fall drunk here,
In this unpleasantly small walled garden.
And, furthermore, that he often used to wake up here,
In this unpleasantly small walled garden.

9 *Drinking Song*
'Hey, little girl: show me your genitalia!
Hey, young woman: show me your genitalia!
Hey, mature matron: show me your genitalia!
Hey, ancient hag: help me down from this tree, will you?'

10

It is sad that the great poet often used to fall drunk here,
In this unpleasantly small walled garden.
And, furthermore, that he often used to wake up, here,
In this even more unpleasantly small walled garden.

11

The absence of birds – the indistinct hills –
The branching supports of wood over the chasm –
The trickle of water – the mutter of labourers –
A deep breath – a window sliding shut –

12

Fog drifts still among the branches
Long after the sun has risen. It drifts on.
Slowly the scholar sits up behind the garden rock.
Well, one thing is certain. It can't still be yesterday, can it?

13

Eyes closed; posture relaxed; serene smile.
Outside his window a quiet road runs quietly.
He was once so very nearly an important man.
Now he so very nearly understands what he did right.

14

Which of the drunken brothers will notice the dead body first,
The crowd wonders, as it watches the stage, agog.
Soon bets begin to be laid on the eventual outcome.
After four hours, excitement has reached fever pitch.

15

A marvellous peak – a second marvellous peak –
A foot trembling at the edge of a chasm –
A second foot trembling at the edge of a chasm –
A third foot trembling at the edge of a chasm –

16

Pensively, the Immortal begins to climb down the lacquer tree.
Hmm. The immediate danger seems to have blown over.
Somehow, he had assumed that this was an uninhabited planet.
He will really need to plan his journeys more carefully in future.

17

At last! At last! A moment of deep incomprehension!
The trim goddess lying on the tavern floor
Has totally forgotten all the Secrets of the Universe!
She begins to play with her body from sheer, unmitigated happiness.

18

It is as if the falling-apart of the Earth
Had been precariously delayed in this tumultuous landscape.
A few vast, hastily assembled mountain rivets
Are holding things together for a few more seconds at most.

19

A few stalks – a few flowers – bird-calls –
A few pauses in the evening's breeze –
There is no particular reason here for happiness –
He turns to watch his wife reading a letter –

20

A massively compassionate figure walks down from the mountain
    retreat.
At last the truth about the human predicament has been revealed to him.
Turning a corner, he trips over a fallen branch lying in the road.
He climbs nimbly to his feet, and continues swiftly down the mountain.

21

Sadly, the man crosses the bridge, followed by his daughter.
She tries to explain to him that it was all a misunderstanding.
He sighs, halts, and throws the monk's penis into the river far below.
Women, eh? Enlightenment, eh? Eh? Not to mention the water.

22

A muddy path in the north of the city
Eventually leads to an overhanging bridge
Which seems to link nowhere with nowhere. An occasional rustle
May be footsteps, but is more probably just trees.

23

The palace dog is feeling a little confused this morning.
It was fed late, and fed by the wrong person.
The wrong person set it free in the wrong garden.
And still no-one has come to fetch it back.

24

The bureaucrat sighs as he adds another column.
Who can possibly be riding so many horses?
He coughs, glancing down from his low pavilion.
Two royal dogs are staring at him insolently.

25

Solemnly he wanders through the autumnal woods,
Outlining his views on immortality
To a silent companion, who, unknown to him,
Seduced his wife twenty-five minutes ago.

26

I trust these three clay actors, excavated together,
Do not exhaust the types available to them.
A judge and two men dressed up as women?
It suggests a certain monotony in the repertoire.

27

The Emperor and his seven lookalikes
Are walking down a palace passageway
On their way to meet the rebel messengers.
Every three or four steps, they exchange places.

28

In this scene from the opera, the sorcerer
Is holding a long, claw-like attachment
Down from the window into the street just below,
Hoping to subtly influence the royal succession.

29

Smiling to himself, the scholar again checks
That the room has everything he will require until sunrise:
Ink, paper, wine, the classic texts,
Five old women, rice, a handful of persimmons.

30

Six sages are standing in a little garden.
Each has shut his eyes, and, by sheer absence of thought,
Has convinced himself that he has been absorbed into the universe.
An enraged servant-girl is about to kick one of them.

31

A few flowers – a few stalks – bird-calls –
A few more pauses in the evening's breeze –
There is no particular reason here for happiness –
He turns to watch his wife pointing at something – and then

32

A sumptuous carpet lies in the garden
Behind the curiously eroded ornamental rock.
There is the imprint of a sleeping form upon it.
The sound of an argument drifts out from the house.

33

A few wet trees line the city lane.
They despatch their loads in occasional flurries.
Since moonlight is not shining on them, no-one is climbing them.
In an hour or so, moonlight will be shining on them.

34

The toys lie scattered and still in the garden.
In their beds, the children move and sleep, sleep and move.
An unseen breeze starts to shift some of the lighter objects.
The children perhaps wake up, but they are soon sleeping again.

35

So much sky visible from a small window.
So many houses available through that small door.
So many pasts in the worn papers in this study.
The scholar stirs briefly during his afternoon nap.

36

When last he visited this city, it was a drab solemn place.
He stayed here for almost a year, and talked to no-one.
Shortly after he left, his illegitimate son was born.
A few weeks later, his second illegitimate son was born.

37 *Drinking Song*

'A further few weeks later, my bastard daughter was born.
A few days later, a third illegitimate son.
The next month, a pair of illegitimate twins.
Ten minutes later, my illegitimate triplets.'

38

The servant hands the scholar his newly acquired scroll, then leaves.
He sits back, sighing happily, and unrolls it piece by piece,
Watching the four seasons pass exquisitely by in front of him.
Somewhat to his surprise, he now reaches a *fifth* section.

39

The lady stands shivering in the snow.
It falls gently onto her, onto the river
Three yards to her left, and onto
The semicircle of soldiers standing round her.

40

'The river,' said the Sage, 'has a great deal to teach all of us.
It does not linger idly in the same place for long.
Nor does it shriek when we enter its bed accidentally.
The sort of mistake which anyone could make in the dark, believe you
    me.'

41

Moonlight – mist – a winding road –
Mist – a running figure – a curve in the road –
Moonlight – a winding road – sweeping mist –
Three leaves swirling along the road – moonlight –

42

Ever since he died, his evenings have been unpredictable,
But his mornings have invariably been the same:
A young lady arrives, bringing him a bowl of tea,
And softly asks him: Do you still not recognise me?

43

'From which we may deduce,' said Avalokiteshvara,
As he was carried feet-first out of the young girl's bedroom,
'That the 54,545 steps towards self-control
Are not susceptible to short-cuts, really.'

44

After forty-one years, the absent-minded Emperor
Has at last mistaken this court lady for his wife.
At once, she imitates the Empress's unique giggle,
With a speed and an accuracy which shock even herself.

45

A flurry of geese takes off from the low lake.
In an hour's time, their flight high overhead
Will enchant two people on a balcony
Which now lies bare, wet, empty, and wind-swept.

46

A scent still lingers about the room.
Darkness is threatened beyond the shutters.
A head on its pillow moves yet again.
First light touches the wet forest.

47

The silence of finished meals returns to the mountainside –
Except for the slapping of the scholars' ink-brushes.
Three men still writing about unreality.
But otherwise a quiet afternoon.

48

Then, after outstripping its tall neighbours on either side,
The central peak stops soaring onwards immediately –
Triumphant, yet gracious with it; unwilling
To humiliate them by showing all it might do.

49

15,493 steps
Lead circuitously upward from this clearing
Towards an inexpressibly beautiful view.
Six steps lead down to a noisy, crowded wineshop.

50 *Drinking Song*

'Folk say there are people by the Western Ocean
Who can do such incredibly clever and talented things.
But can they do this? Or this? Or this? Or this?'
(This song is always performed with forthright and memorable
    gestures.)

51

A few bamboo stems sway unimportantly in the wind.
There are three, or four – possibly five of them altogether.
No. To be quite accurate: there are six of them.
No, wait a moment – there are seven of them.

52

An insect of enormous complexity
Walks down a plant of enormous complexity,
Over a cold hand of enormous complexity,
And onto a really rather simple document.

53

The clouds are rolling like an avalanche
Above the city, hardly noticed by anyone.
In fact, a tremendous storm has already begun
Over a nearby lake. It quivers in that branch.

54

A laughing priest is passing by underneath a tree,
On his way to commit an appalling indecency.
Or perhaps he has committed the act already.
It is difficult to be quite sure, with all this foliage about.

55

The bureaucrat sighs as he adds up another column.
Who can possibly be riding so many horses?
He coughs again, and glances down from his low pavilion.
A fragrant breeze blows through the empty garden.

56

For three unbroken hours before her marriage
She is given information on sexual matters
By an aunt whom she has never seen before,
And whom she takes considerable care to avoid afterwards.

57

How little the shrimp thought at dawn, shrugged by the sea,
In its cold, legendary, saline indifference,
That fifteen pairs of hands would have touched it by the evening,
Before it was hurled with a yell of contempt over a garden wall.

58

He stops for an instant as he crosses the bridge.
A thin torrent courses by underneath him.
Why should he remember an unliked aunt at just this moment?
He was expected in the palace half an hour ago.

59

The connoisseur gazes, rapt, at the picture in front of him.
For several decades, he has burned with desire to own it.
And now, at last, it is his! Here it is in front of him!
But why is thin rain falling on this glorious morning too?

60

Rain beats on the exposed hill
Above a couple of sodden, neighbourly roofs.
Under one, a husband and wife sit in silence.
Under the other, a husband and wife sit in silence.

61

An accidental tuft of grass waves on the palace roof;
Unseen by the third emperor, the fourth
Emperor, the fifth emperor, and even by the sixth
Emperor, whose fleeing foot disturbs it.

62

A standing tablet set up in a courtyard
To commemorate a spectacular long-past victory
Topples over onto the ground, alarming
A passing monk who is thinking about illusion.

63

A vast army is hectically engaged
In dragging some of the Great Wall southwards for greater safety.
An act of choice, perhaps; but the neutral observer
Has to call this a moral victory for the barbarians.

64

Enamelled trees grow by the river.
A delicate humanity close their jewelled doors
And sail gently downstream towards the palaces
Where the worst of the loud screams have been heard coming from.

65

The horses run in straight lines through the lost years,
Stopping only a few million times in front of
Ordinary houses, bridges, gates, before
Dispersing throughout the huge, waterlogged plains.

66

This small high bridge in the centre of Paradise
Is the perfect place from which to observe the universe.
From this vantage-point, everything becomes coherent.
How strange that it can be unoccupied for so long.

67

The edge of the cliff – the edge of the waterfall –
The edge of sense – the edge of twilight –
Ah well; we can stay here; I can stay here, or go –
The permanent, ever-changing edge of the waterfall –

68

Some men are building the foundations of a pavilion
At the edge of a lake. Their crude ringing hammers
And shouted orders are the loud prelude
To a drifting half-century of leisured sighs.

69

After a week or so, the great religious thinker
Suffers a momentary lapse in concentration;
Allowing the singing-girls to leap up off the mattress,
And run away to safety through the unguarded door.

70

A field full of decapitated soldiers
Must be a grim sight, the historian reflects
As he glances up from his reading, over the balcony
To where his young sons are shouting in the garden.

71

The bureaucrat sighs as he adds up another column.
Who can possibly still be riding so many horses?
This is just as boring as his previous life was.
Why did he ask to be sent back to what he already knew?

72

After five minutes, the Goddess abandons her task.
When she returns to the restaurant later in the evening,
She has managed to acquire from somewhere an exquisite cleavage.
Triumphantly, she out-stares the restaurant-keeper's wife.

73

'No,' said the Master, at the foot of a tall ladder,
The top of which vanished out of sight into the clouds:
'There is no such thing as a simple way into heaven.
We had this same argument down in the brothel. Remember?'

74

The priest thinks hard, and then begins to write.
He pours out reason after reason after reason after reason
For disregarding the evidence of the senses.
The females tied to his bed begin to whimper.

75

Avoiding the rain, he hurries over to a doorway beside the road.
Half-heartedly he examines a nearer part of the wall.
He hears a thud, and a puzzling cry behind the door.
He shifts his feet, sighs, and hurries back into the downpour.

76

Obviously the final day of autumn.
The last possible leaf is about to fall.
The last possible goose is about to enter the air.
The last boat is about to be left where it is.

77

Mountain mist – village – riverside houses –
Light from somewhere else – rain sweeping the water –
That sound – like a high fence being torn apart –
Rain sweeping along the path – more urgent voices –

78

Who is moving about in the room above?
He lies, unsleeping, in a house beside the river.
He will leave for ever in the first light of morning.
The footsteps stop. He hears the river brimming.

79

A thin, empty road is leading quietly up a hill.
There must have been a thousand such since we left the capital.
Why should we wish so strongly to discover where this one leads to?
We are in too much of a hurry always on too few roads.

80 *Drinking Song*
'And if, my dear, I had not stopped at this wine-house,
But had gone on instead to the next wine-house,
I would either now not be singing this song,
Or would be only a thin sound you could just hear in the distance.'

81

Fences and leaves serve almost to hide the house.
The man inside it pulls tightly around himself
The loose-fitting robe which he always wears when alone.
So calm an afternoon, to be a hopelessly final one.

82

The sound of the wall crackling behind him
Restores him to a consciousness of the situation.
He opens his eyes, and again contemplates the flames.
Damn! It's *still* not happening to someone else.

83

Solemnly he wanders through the autumnal woods,
Outlining his views on immortality
To a silent companion who, unknown to him,
Is carrying a heavy metal bar in his sleeve.

84

The Emperor is walking down a tunnel
Which links, as he rightly thinks, his private apartments
With the rooms of a young lady he is particularly fond of.
Another two or three days should get him there.

85

The two scholars walk down a road away from the palace,
Discussing what they had expected from life in their youth.
As they cross a bridge, they are passed by a calm gentleman
Who was expected in the same building several years ago.

86

The Ghost trudges wearily back to the palace.
Already it can hear, (as it were) in imagination,
The raucous laughter that will greet his return.
He must have been mad, to have followed a fly such a distance.

87

How could anyone who lived in such a building ever be overthrown?
Would there not always be another room, another floor, where he
    could hide?
A whole raging army could disappear in search of him.
Every second hour, a soldier might glimpse an ambiguous figure in the
    distance.

88

The bureaucrat sighs as he adds up another column.
Who can possibly be riding so many horses?
He sighs, and glances down from his low pavilion.
Three and a half royal dogs are staring at him insolently.

89

The old man creeps towards the shaded doorway,
Furtively looking to left and right.
He goes in through the entrance and is lost to sight.
The sun continues its slow, silent game with shadows.

90

A window open above a lane.
A cat or two climbing over the walls.
A noise which is rather difficult to interpret.
A silence which is utterly ordinary.

91

This small bridge in the corner of Paradise
Has (roughly) 896 billion names carved upon it.
It is in a remote spot, and is thus rarely visited.
And most who do visit, obey the tiny *Do Not Deface* sign.

92 *Fragment*

When the Master happened to look in through a window
Of a house we were passing in a quiet suburban lane,
And saw a young maid charmingly playing with herself,
He sighed and said: 'By *right belief*, I mean . . .'

93

The greatest forger in China wakens up one morning
Into a curiously bright implausible sunlight.
There is something slightly too chilled about the sunlight.
He looks down into his garden from slightly too great a height.

94

The river laps against the stone steps,
Laps again against the stone steps,
Fails to lap against the stone steps,
Then again laps again against the stone steps.

95

Sunset seeps into the garden of the great poet,
Imparting a magnificent calmness to the lawn;
From where, if one were listening attentively,
One could just make out the sounds of someone writing.

96

In the garden of the imperial household, an obviously pristine stone.
A stone untouched perhaps for four centuries.
The wind shifts and re-shifts the blossoming branches;
But the bright sun never quite finds a gap, does it? Does it?

97

Passing through the forty-first consecutive courtyard,
One suddenly realises that the emperor
Might well have been that nondescript old man
Talking benignly to flowers in the twenty-seventh.

98

The Emperor pauses in his laboured ascent of the sacred mountain.
He opens another bottle of his favourite wine.
He makes unmistakable gestures towards a particular concubine.
Prudently, the priests turn and acclaim a dreary sunset.

99
A candle flickers below a tall vase.
Outside, it is all darkness and the occasional traveller.
Inside, it is almost darkness, and two people smiling.
The flame dances and shakes; shakes; dances and shakes.

100
The bridge crashes into the water –
The wall crashes into the water –
The sky crashes into the water –
The water begins to drain away.

Book Two

Darkness and the Occasional Traveller

101

Will he get home before winter finally arrives?
After all, his house is merely across that bridge.
Surely there is no need for him to hurry?
The trees are still autumnal. Why is he hurrying?

102

A man is running along by a lake in the dead of winter.
Although the middle of the day, it is still dark.
But not as dark as the darkness in his mind.
Life continues normally in all but one of the village houses.

103

The traveller is angry. The huge valley
Lying before him is blatantly unnecessary.
But for that, he would already be home, as promised.
His wife for some reason sighs in a neighbour's garden.

104 *Fragment*

When the Master was treacherously stopped at the frontiers of Chu
By an over-zealous customs official, he dismounted,
Sat down with us by the side of the road and whispered,
'If either of those bound, gagged, old crones are discovered . . .'

105

The great poet puzzles over the text produced while he was drunk.
He sips a bowl of wine, trying to understand it.
He sips another bowl of wine, trying to understand it.
By now, he is beginning to understand it.

106

Sunrise seeps into the garden of the great poet,
Imparting a magnificent colour to the lawn;
From where, if one were listening attentively,
One could just make out the sounds of someone being sick.

107

The great poet puzzles over the text he produced when drunk.
He scratches his head, trying to understand it.
He goes out for a walk, trying to understand it.
He hurries back home and hides, having just understood it.

108

As he leaves the astrologer's house, delighted to have been told
That all the signs favour his immediate journey to the capital,
He trips over a garden rock, falls, and breaks both legs.
He crawls back into the house, to check one or two details.

109

The scholar's son has just uttered his first word.
His mother is slumped in a dead faint on the carpet.
His father is leafing through the Sixty Volume Dictionary,
Feverishly searching for a plausible excuse.

110

The two little boys stand with their foreheads touching.
It is an idyllic moment in a garden.
While, in a small room, barely five steps away,
Something much more crude and adult altogether is happening.

111

The civilized man with the head of a large green ferret
Discovers that the door has been accidentally left unlocked.
Surely then, it should be possible for him to wander through the palace?
He looks carefully round the door, uncertain in his mind.

112

And so one's whole life passes in a foreign country.
The eyes water; the air suddenly seems poured from another jar.
The laughing inhabitants of the brain are all in reality forty years older
    now.
These absurd decisions! My father shouting. The brilliance of a
    stream or a phrase.

113

The view is not so much of higher mountains behind high mountains
As of a second planet pressed close against our earth.
We are within half a second of annihilation.
I'll not even have time to look at your face again.

114

1395 appeals to the imperial horses,
And the sun too is something they are clearly in favour of.
Their drumming hooves dislocate the soft grass.
Yes, this spring air is just the right size for all of them.

115

The man taking wood downriver in a small boat
For the third time that morning, looks across
And sees that the wine-drinkers are still carousing near the bank.
But, on his return journey, they have at last disappeared.

116

The Goddess locks the door, and turns round, smiling.
The elderly sage, cowering in the corner, whimpers
As she walks tenderly towards him, licking her lips.
He had never dreamt enlightenment would be *quite* like this.

117

As the scroll about enlightenment unfolds, the handwriting
Becomes less and less decipherable, until
A single stuttering unbroken line
Unrolls for hours before the mesmerized sage.

118

As the acolyte bows before him, the Zen master,
Wishing to shock him into enlightenment,
Raps him sharply on the ear with a begging-bowl.
With magnificent aplomb, the disciple brings out a sledgehammer.

119 *Fragment*

When the Master fell badly ill at the boundaries of Liao,
And all of us feared for his life, and he was asked
If any of his past actions still troubled his conscience,
He groaned and answered: If only those five or six murders . . .

120 *Fragment*

When the Master was asked, how did he reconcile
His insistence on the need for a chaste, virtuous life
With his well-known penchant for having large servant-girls
Sit down on his face, he replied: Although *at first sight* . . .

121

The man who has almost reached the top of the mountain
Is also the man strolling beside a stream
Immediately below, not far from a precipice.
Curiously, both of them are walking uphill.

122
A few roofs show among the pines,
Seeming slightly higher than they were last year.
Voices drift over the roadside travellers,
Seeming slightly louder than they were last year.

123
Land visible among the wisps of mist.
A tree leans out from a rockface.
A flood of water pours from a cleft.
Mist visible among the wisps of mist.

124
Is someone ahead of him on the path?
The area is notorious for footpads;
And dusk is setting in. He has often wondered
What it must be like to be a footpad. Hmm.

125
A donkey shifts its position in front of a door.
It shifts its position in front of a door again.
Again it shifts its position in front of a door.
The door is not opened. Or has it been? I suspect not.

126
It is dark and deserted at the mountain pass.
A clump of snow-covered trees seems to guard it.
Is it merely the snow which gives them that luminous appearance?
Well, yes; it is. It is. What else could it be?

127
Through the trees at the side of his neighbour's house,
A falling pass with a vast town lying below it.
Through the trees at the side of his own house,
A fascinating view of a high wooden fence.

128 *Drinking Song*
'What though my neighbours have vistas of mountains and valleys,
A broad river, and the roofs of a picturesque city,
While I have only a view of a couple of trees, and a window?
After all, it was me who had the first choice of these houses.'

129

The leaves turn this way and that.
A hidden being runs among the branches.
The leaves turn this way and that, this way and that.
Something is standing motionless within the branches.

130

A branch swaying – three sparrows – a branch swaying –
One sparrow – a branch swaying – no sparrows –
A branch swaying – a swaying branch – a branch calm –
A branch swaying – one hundred and seventeen sparrows.

131

A leaf is floating on the surface of the vanished lake
Which wholly covered this central plain of China
During part of its oceanic past. A summer's breeze
Has blown it to a great height for a few moments.

132

Throughout the country, buffaloes drawing ploughs;
Minor officials sharpening their steely looks;
Grotesque numbers who are dying; grotesquer numbers who are not.
And very few historians pausing very long for thought.

133

The dead man's hand reaches out of the water,
But snatches nothing, except for a passing fly.
It returns slowly to somewhere below the surface.
No: that is not anger, whatever else it might be.

134

So much sky – so much distance – so much trouble –
We must leave the house immediately leave the house –
A gate clicks that we shall never close again –
A bird flies off in a fright – the road at once crowded –

135

After an hour spent admiring the river,
The philosopher turns reluctantly to leave.
Can it really all have happened here nearly fifty years ago?
He picks something up from the ground, and hurries away.

136

An old man is visible in the open doorway.
The traveller gazes through the open doorway,
Then continues his journey towards the mist-filled mountains.
The old man turns slowly, and looks over at the door.

137

A pagoda nestles among the fir-trees.
A precarious arched bridge spans the churning pool.
The bronze gate of the Temple of Harmony swings open for a
    moment.
No-one enters or leaves, and it slowly swings back shut.

138

The wife of the most important man in the neighbourhood
Meets him, on a small path through the forest.
Such a trivial, narrow, dangerous, herb-gatherer's path!
He leans aside, smiling dubiously, to let her pass.

139

Observing how the wind makes the bamboo stalk
Strike repeatedly sometimes at the wall behind it,
The scholar looks up, and watches the bamboo stalk
Sometimes strike repeatedly at the wall behind it.

140

The Emperor is walking down a tunnel
Which links (or so he thinks) his secret apartments
With the rooms of a young woman he is particularly fond of.
Another two or three weeks should get him there.

141

Are the four thousand women in the palace today
The same as the four thousand who were here yesterday?
That would be an extraordinary coincidence,
Considering how many doors have been opening and shutting.

142

The Emperor is walking down a corridor again,
Which links (or so he thinks) his secret apartments
With the room of a young woman he is particularly fond of.
This time he *has* remembered to bring the key.

143 *Drinking Song*

'Tonight, the clouds are a few hard straight lines above us.
The upper storeys lie in hard straight lines over our heads.
The road in the distance is a hard straight line fading fast.
And now is not the moment to whine about the past.'

144

The wife of the most important man in the neighbourhood
Meets him on a small path through the forest.
Such a trivial, narrow, dangerous, herb-gatherer's path!
He steps aside, bowing politely, to let her pass. And – whoops!

145

The two ambassadors meet on the mist-filled road.
They stop for a while, and exchange laughing anecdotes
About bad food, sunsets, and weeping servant-girls.
Then, sighing, they continue homewards with their defiant insults.

146

The Immortals have captured a human being!
They escort her up a path, chattering triumphantly –
And notice too late that she seems to have escaped.
They loiter at a sudden corner, baffled and accusatory.

147

There are 36 chief faults to be avoided
When painting Gods, according to the books.
But true artists need commit to memory
Only rule 37: Paint Something Else.

148

This scholar-painter is famous throughout Wu for his austerity.
He never uses one more brush-stroke than is absolutely necessary.
He will never so much as speak a single superfluous word.
Friends often gaze in speechless wonder at his seventeen daughters.

149

He wakens up in the middle of the night,
To discover that a large, sharp-clawed lizard
Is not standing beside him, licking its lips.
He rises and walks around the garden for an hour or so.

150

The phrase floats upward from the winding pathway
To the raised pavilion where he sits, drinking.
'I'll tell you what I miss most about impotence – '
Intrigued, he leans forward, but already they have gone.

151

Rain beats on the exposed hill
Above a couple of sodden, neighbourly roofs.
Beneath one, a woman is kissing her daughter's little nose.
Beneath the other, a man is kissing his mother-in-law's bigger nose.

152

The acrobat leaps again and the crowds gasp.
Is there no end to his talents, they ask themselves.
He leaps up onto one of the roofs above them.
He jumps again, and they utterly lose sight of him.

153

There are jellyfish on the branches of a tree,
On one of the avenues leading to the conjuror's house.
The sea has been receding steadily for weeks.
From inside a cormorant's brain, he watches them doubtfully.

154

The Emperor is running along a tunnel
Which links (or so he thinks) his most private apartments
With the room of a young woman he is particularly fond of.
Another two or three months should get him there.

155

Such a breadth of land revealed from the hilltop.
One may look down, and see a tapping foot,
In its fashionable footgear, on unfashionable rocks,
Or look up to see a skyline four days' distant.

156

Some young, some old,
A crowd of ladies drifts down a palace corridor.
A few seconds later,
A crowd of young girls swarms up the same corridor.

157

The wounded recluse who recently settled in a villa,
With no company except a handful of mirrors
And a set of pretty well-behaved identical female quads
Has lately rediscovered his naïve belief in the Gods.

158 *A Political Allegory*

'I seem to have returned to this ordinary pool again.
I am far from certain why I keep returning to it.
Surely the reflection of a few of last year's clouds
Is not enough to draw me back so repeatedly?'

159

A narrow path runs from the door of the small riverside house.
It runs through a fenceless garden and crosses a bridge.
It runs through a wood, then crosses another bridge.
It continues through the fields towards a bigger road.

160

Even on apparent mountain-tops there are cliff-faces,
Leading with one last thrust to yet greater height.
One could never be a mountaineer in landscapes like this.
One would never be sure one had no choice but to descend.

161

The Goddess, taken by surprise in the dead man's kitchen
At his sudden resurrection, smiles disarmingly,
And prepares for him her first ever attempt at a fish soup.
She has stopped smiling when she starts her second attempt.

162

Rain clings to the tall weeds by the river,
Trickling or falling downwards under the pressure
Of the newly arriving droplets, towards the roadway
On which the Emperor's favourite horse stands bleeding.

163

The messenger knocks furiously at the door.
Snow drops from the pinetrees on the mountain-tops.
The messenger knocks even more furiously at the door.
More snow drops from the pinetrees on the mountain-tops.

164

No-one is on the bridge and no boat is in the lake.
The valley is totally empty.
A fire is burning behind a distant forest.
No-one is fleeing from the fire. At last.

165

This particular path is rather peculiar.
It starts off narrow, veers to the left,
Widens, goes through an archway, splits into two,
And becomes, without warning, both a stairway and a cliff.

166

A lock-up lies directly through the wall
From the garden where the great flower-painter
Crouches over a rare chrysanthemum.
He moans at the sight of a few perfect fallen petals.

167

A standing tablet set up in a courtyard
To commemorate a spectacular long-past victory
Topples over onto the ground, alarming
Two passers-by who are languidly discussing history.

168

With blood pouring from a multitude of wounds,
He bursts out from among some sheltering trees,
Staggers moaning towards the dumbfounded villagers,
Carries on past them, and disappears round a corner.

169

An argument in nineteenth-century Chinese
About a poet of the seventh century
Wakens up a baby whom a nurse is carrying
In the opposite direction, over a thirteenth-century bridge.

170

The Emperor is haring up a tunnel
Which links (or so he thinks) to his private apartments
The retreat of a young woman he is particularly fond of.
Another two or three years should see him there.

171

A couple of Gods are staring at the horizon
In that way Gods have of staring when disconsolate.
The expression in their eyes might almost be human
Were it not for the fact that their faces are invisible.

172

Clouds cut across the waists of the high pines.
Above them, a man is asleep on a mountain slope.
Above that, more cloud hovers, thin as a rope.
Above this, a God is trying to un-knot eternity, and failing.

173

The contorted pine-tree apparently changes its mind
Five or six times between the cluster of rocks
And the fullness of the air. Its topmost branches
Sway calmly in the wrong part of the sky.

174

As the decades pass, the old tree
Takes on a more and more menacing appearance.
Slowly the path around it
Approaches nearer and nearer to the dark wall.

175

The lake shimmers.
The two men talk.
Willows sway.
Water swirls and gurgles beneath the wooden floor they are seated
  upon.

176

So, the man who sold them the wine was not lying after all!
It really does have the effect which he claimed it would have.
Hurriedly the buyers disperse homewards, eager
To be seen by their loved ones before they return to normal.

177

It is the morning of the day when the qufas are due to open!
In house after house the sunlight is greeted with joy.
The afternoon is awash with voices.
The evening is still awash with voices.

178

Beautiful flute music is distilled throughout the palace.
One may wander down the hallways for a whole day
And seem to come no nearer to its source,
And seem to go no further from its source.

179

The fields where those stallions are running in delight
Were the execution grounds of the old Han capital.
The horses weave deliriously left and right and right,
As if trying to throw off intense, invisible riders.

180

In a ripple of a treeless, riverless plain,
A hunter is tying his quarry to his horse.
She struggles tearfully with the ropes, insisting
That she is really only a *terribly minor* Goddess.

181

The scholars glance about themselves.
Surely this is the perfect opportunity?
Quickly they secrete themselves in various parts of the corridor.
A very tall servant-girl steps warily round the corner.

182

The tree is large, yet the bird upon it is larger.
The man sleeping below it moans, but does not wake up.
One of his daughters, in a light-filled kitchen,
Is nimbly removing feathers from a pair of tired wings.

183

The physician must wait patiently for the mystic
To return to the earth from his spiritual journey;
Before attempting to cure his painful, chronic condition
By expertly applying a burning stick to his anus.

184

A pilgrim, who may be either male or female,
Is being spoken to on a mountain pathway
By a child who may be either real or imaginary.
It is either spring or autumn. The sun is out.

185

With blood seeping from a multitude of wounds,
He bursts out from among some cruelly sheltering trees,
Staggers moaning towards dumbfounded villagers,
Warns them about life, and collapses, at last dead.

186

The bloodstained Bodhisattva peeps out from behind the door.
Perfectly ordinary people are walking down the street beyond.
Can he manage to make his gory way off through them, unnoticed?
Even a sacred hatred of actors may be over-indulged, it seems.

187

Hearing of the defeat, the actor sinks to the ground, groaning.
Sobbing once or twice, he reaches into his superb gown,
Pulls out his penis, and indolently begins to tug at it.
A ripple of alarm stirs among the cognoscenti.

188

The crowd gasps at the latest turn of events on stage.
The villain tears off the thin young woman's bodice,
To discover that the wearer is in fact the vanished old judge.
There follows an unforgettable 25-minute laugh.

189

The crowd gazes in rapture towards the stage.
A huge, hairy man lifts an axe above his cranium,
Thereby conclusively proving he is no longer in Korea.
Humbled and terrified, the prostitute hides her armpits.

190

The crowd roars at the incredible denoument!
The old judge triple somersaults in at one window,
Bounces head first off the buttocks of the floored villain,
Collects the young girl, and flies on out the other window.

191

The sound of the lute – the sound of the guitar –
Or something like – singing voices – laughter – the sound
Of valuable old instruments being gleefuly maltreated –
More laughter – footsteps – welcoming voices – uproar –

192
Moonlight on the glittering stream
Running by the closed wooden doors.
People are sleeping very near here.
And some are moving in a dream.

193
All day the unrelenting rain
Has fallen unrelentingly
Onto the garden where they should be sitting
Exchanging childhood reminiscences.

194
Tumultuous rain is falling throughout the night.
The drought has ended. Boisterous streams
Pick rediscovered pathways between houses
Where their tributaries bubble inside unmemorable dreams.

195
Moonlight on the guttering stream
Running by the closed wooden doors.
People are sleeping very near here.
People are awake very near here.

196
Tumultuous rain is falling throughout the night.
The drought has ended. Boisterous streams
Pick rediscovered pathways between houses,
Mingling their murmurs with those of sighing spouses.

197
Tumultuous rain is falling throughout the night.
The drought has ended. Boisterous streams
Pick rediscovered pathways between houses
Making the next world for the next light.

198
No-one is present in the vast courtyard.
No-one is looking up at the breaking clouds.
No-one is worriedly pacing up and down
Waiting for news from the beleagered town.

199
Children are playing furiously in a garden.
The noise of a nearby battle does not quite reach them.
The voices of their parents reach them from time to time.
It is all several centuries ago anyway. Seven, at least.

200
At last, evening settles in among the rich fruit-trees,
Having for so long been kept at bay
By music, laughter, mutual expressions of affection,
Of fondness, of love, of reluctance, of parting, of silence.

Book Three

Waking Up in One of the Pavilions of Heaven

201 *Drinking Song*

'One man writes in a study. Two women
Talk on a balcony. Three ferrymen
Help four passengers ashore. Five tutors
Cross six bridges, followed by seven children . . .'

202

Some terrified dancing-girls are standing motionless.
Some guards are bustling in through a magnificent door.
A severed head or two drops rather blatantly to the floor.
The reconciliation attempt has not, it seems, been a great success.

203

Why is he waiting in the audience hall of the temple,
Wearing such a strained, anxious expression?
After all, he is fairly certain that none of the Gods exist.
Hidden behind a screen, a tiny dog is checking a list.

204 *Drinking Song*

'. . . while 93 customers sit in 94 restaurants,
Looking up from 95 bowls with 96 prawns in them,
To observe 97 men run down 98 flights of 99 steps,
Pursued by a hundred soldiers, while 101 onlookers . . .'

205

The old woman holds high up above her head her frail arms,
At the end of which extends a huge leaden cauldron,
Wherein a large, panting soldier stands, fondling her charms.
In a quavering voice, she starts to sing, to attract attention.

206

The holy man falling down the mountainside,
Scrabbling for handholds, hitting ledge after ledge,
Has reached an impressively materialistic mode of thinking
By the time he reaches the river, and topples over the edge.

207 *Drinking Song*

'Abnormal? What do you mean, "abnormal"? Me?
Is it abnormal to like to watch your daughters
Licking the reflections of their tongues in the mirror?
What? Oh, sorry. I thought it was me you were talking to.'

208 *Drinking Song*

'Oh, is it abnormal to like to watch your daughters
Licking the reflections of their tongues in the mirror,
While your neighbour's wife shyly sticks her own tongue into your
    ear?
To be honest, I sometimes worry that I might be a little queer.'

209

The shape of the mountain lake lying far below him
Surprises the cautiously downward peering traveller.
He laughs, and looks down again, to check he is not wrong.
Then, for only the second time in his life, he bursts into song.

210

The robber has passed by; the man
Reclining luxuriously beside the river
Will never know how close he came to losing the taste of this wine.
He pours out another drink, and sighs contentedly.

211 *Drinking Song*

'Why, you ask, am I lying here drunk on this grass verge?
Don't you realise that the rebels arrived long ago,
And have been hiding for years behind the houseplants,
Waiting for the right moment at which to emerge? No?'

212

The naked Goddess turns over on her side,
And tumbles off the oven-bed, onto the floor.
Quickly she glances up. Has she wakened him?
She smiles to re-encounter his low, devoted snore.

213

Two women run down the pathway, smiling.
Twenty-five seconds later, a stately, distinguished man
Runs down the pathway. He is smiling too.
Then silence returns to the rather humdrum view.

214

The morning sun has thrown onto the wall
The shadows of a thousand moving people.
A door opens and closes in a courtyard.
A rustling sound travels down the long street and disappears.

215

The butterfly, newly awakened, refreshed by sleep,
Flutters into the bedroom of the philosopher.
Have I, it wonders, ever been here before?
Why do these slippers seen so curiously familiar?

216 *Drinking Song*

'The fruits hang from the branch like small perfect moons.
In the middle of the morning, a hand reaches up and takes one.
Why does it ever occur to us that we have been here before?
Someone feeds on our misery, and throws away the core.'

217

The mistress and the maid have exchanged clothes.
They sit in the darkened room, sniggering quietly.
At length a heavy tread approaches the door –
The master! Or, certainly someone wearing his slippers.

218 *Drinking Song*

'The sage, peering through the thickening mist,
Sees a friend approaching on his garden path.
Damn! And just as one is about to have a bath
With the pretty servant one has finally managed to get pissed!'

219 *Drinking Song*

'Yes, that is the judge's house over there on the right.
No. That is not really one of his cousins
Who is standing in the balcony doorway, dancing and giggling.
Yes. That is probably the judge's arm which has just yanked her out
    of sight.'

220 *Drinking Song*

'What is the point of living forever without *her*? [Pointing.]
What is the point of living forever without *her*? [Pointing.]
What is the point of living forever without *her*? [Pointing.]'
(This song becomes unbearable in a really crowded room.)

221 *Drinking Song*

'I found myself at the top of a vertiginously high cliff,
Far above the river which I was sauntering by ten seconds before.
So what could I do but walk back down again?'
(Here everyone makes a suggestion, and the least obscene contributor
    is thrown out into the street.)

222 *Drinking Song*

'. . . and one thousand two hundred and fifty-five classics scholars
Read by the light of one thousand two hundred and fifty-six
    candles.
While one thousand two hundred and fifty-seven women
Gaze at them with innumerable emotions . . .'

223

By climbing out among the branches in his garden,
And inching his way with pained fingers along a high rough wall,
He is able to catch sight of her, seated on her balcony –
If she has bothered to come out and sit on her balcony.

224

The lady lifts her head thoughtfully.
The man lifts his head thoughtfully.
The evening clouds float thoughtfully
Above the thoughtfully quiet lane.

225

Dark clouds group and regroup beyond the passes.
Lights on the river flicker, dip, and flicker.
Surely this afternoon is just too heavy for the earth?
Surely it will never shake off such a dead weight upon it?

226

Carefully he cleans the shrine to his dead wife.
All the lovirgly treasured relics are still there.
All the combs; all the clothes; all the trinkets; all the fading scents.
Almost the sense that those approaching footsteps might even be hers.

227

He is finally woken up by the loud knocking at the door.
Wiping the sleep from his eyes, he strides towards it –
And finds himself face to face with his long-lost wife.
They embrace heartily, which wakens his wife up.

228

Two philosophers sit under old trees by the river,
Discussing the strange way women address each other.
After an hour, they have become silent.
After two hours, they have become even silenter.

229

Mist breathes among the trees in the strangely bright valley.
A philosopher walks quietly up a slope
Behind a young woman whom he is trying to keep in sight.
The chances of his doing so for ever are, of course, slight.

230

In the evening, he sits in a pavilion by a bridge,
Expecting that his wine-jug will, of course, be empty eventually,
And that neither pavilion nor bridge nor jug shall suddenly collapse.
However, it proved to be a not entirely predictable evening.

231

And now the annual river ceremony commences.
A grinning, malicious crone walks towards the river bank,
Expecting to push in the two nude virgins trembling at the edge.
However, this year some long overdue changes have been introduced.

232

Women are walking through his memory
As he lies drowsing in his lakeside pavilion.
How many rooms are there in his memory?
A further door closes with each sigh.

233

That small bridge takes one into another province.
That other small bridge leads into a third province.
About ten million people in each province at the moment.
No-one, just at the moment, on either of the bridges.

234

By the time the old man emerges from the pavilion,
He has thought, in all, of perhaps a dozen women.
Ah, if he had the chance again, he would do it all so differently!
He slaps his head, and stumbles back for a forgotten wine-jar.

235 *Drinking Song*

'This small thicket of bamboo along the riverbank, just here,
Would give us the perfect cover from behind which to frown upon
Those deplorable goings-on in the private pleasure-boats,
Were it not that the river – damn them all! damn! – had been
    redirected last year.'

236 *Drinking Song*
'A quiet mist rises from the floor of the forest.
The furthermost trees almost appear to be retreating.
Who can explain to us why our hearts are beating?
What? Aren't they beating? That's odd. They *should* be beating.'

237 *Drinking Song*
'What laughter behind that gate! Are we worthy? Are we fit?
We knock on the locked door, but no small charmer answers it.
Somebody climbs the wall, and calls out from far above:
"Oh! This garden is full of beings not falling in love!"'

238 *Drinking Song*
'The government official, sitting in his garden,
Was sitting utterly motionless in his garden.
Absolutely, totally and utterly motionless.
So I gave him back his father's truss and said, I beg your pardon.'

239 *Drinking Song*
'Oh, the traveller rides swiftly up to the inn door,
Tosses some babies into the house, and departs.
The chatter of the denizens continues unabated.
No-one remembers often enough how madly we were created.'

240 *Drinking Song*
'. . . while one million, five hundred and twenty-seven thousand,
Four hundred and twenty-eight priests utter the names
Of one million, five hundred and twenty-seven thousand,
Four hundred and twenty-nine peerless Gods in their prayers . . .'

241 *Drinking Song*
'This autumn evening, the river valley is particularly mournful.
Most of the willow trees hereabout have corpses hanging from them.
No; I exaggerate. Only four or five have corpses hanging from them.
Well, okay, actually *none* have – but it *is* raining heavily.'

242
A column of dead men line the long wide road
Which runs monotonously by a long wide river,
Watching a column of bejewelled ships glide past.
A few scuffles break out, but they rarely last.

243

The swaying road is not interested in the next town.
He is carrying his load like a beast of burden.
Should he not have better things to do with his life?
Well . . . he disappears in any case; whether he has or not.

244 *Epitaph*

'We loved him as our servants love the fire.
He held door after door open, and we went confidently through them.
He closed one door, and we waited in vain on the other side.
The cause of his slight limp we never thought to enquire.'

245

A pallid official hurries up the stairway,
To plead with the Emperor to postpone his planned invasion
After the worst omen imaginable.
Someone has just dropped dead in the Temple of Everlasting Youth.

246

The Goddess's face is slowly splitting open.
The other people in the tavern gaze over at her in horror.
A crack runs down her forehead, then on into her cheek.
Someone has badly misinformed her about laughter.

247

How the leaves switch delicately this way and that.
The road to the palace lies across the swollen stream.
He was expected there at least an hour ago.
How the leaves delicately switch, that way and this.

248

They say, fruit was once kept in this dish;
Hand after hand picked fruit out of this dish;
We may imagine, if we wish, I suppose, Watteau or someone else's
    ever contemporaneous hand ever commencing yet another drawing,
    probably of a nude woman, for they say he was distinctly partial to
    that sort of thing, and who can blame him?
However, even if we do not, in limpid rooms within sight of a road
    flowing in a Chinese manner, or a river ditto, or perhaps both, fruit
    was often, in varying quantities, fairly thoughtlessly, being taken
    out of this dish. Is that not so?

249

Yes, at last; the thousand millionth fly to be devoured by that
    particular type of finch;
I speak, of course, only of those within the vast and ever-changing
    territory of China;
It happens, if considerations of relativity permit, outside a small shop,
    which there are only two people inside, discussing the news of the
    insurrection;
It flies off at once to the neighbouring house, and lands among some
    recently abandoned household utensils.

250

Each morning, the court lady goes down to the river,
Which flows with imperturbable nonchalance
Among the imperial walls and halls. Her purpose
Is an obscure one, quite unknown to anyone. Next!

251

A non-existent moon is shining on a garden.
A few people are talking in low voices
In the opposite of human communication.
As they fade away, others take their places.

252

A strange bluish glow illuminates the mountain,
Although the surroundings contain ten sorts of darkness;
And unexpected people are walking through the gloom,
Who claim to have something vague to do with transience.

253

Meanwhile, in another part of the scroll,
The man who was so messily decapitated
Is seated on a mossy, airy riverbank,
Arguing heatedly with an apparently smiling friend.

254

Waking up in one of the pavilions of heaven,
He is in no landscape that he can recognise.
Quiet trees; house; a lane; a throbbing river –
He smiles to see so subtle a paradise.

255

A small path meanders by the pavilion
Where a man sits, playing a friendly game like bowls
With the fresh morning mist – a notoriously difficult
Opponent to beat by strictly legal means.

256

All this love, and much besides, has vanished into the ground.
And little more can be brought back than the chance cup
Which his lips touched, or a vase stroked by her fingers.
But most love has disappeared much deeper even than that.

257

Beneath these two trees lies the very spot
Where one thousand years ago a crucial battle-plan was conceived.
A modest stranger quietly emerges from behind them.
Sighing with renewed contentment, he continues his lazy journey.

258

Rain beats upon the exposed hill
Above a couple of sodden, neighbourly roofs.
Under one, a mother is singing her children to sleep.
Under the other, a man is trying to waken his wife up.

259

With suspicious nonchalance, the delicate young lady
Looks at the huge insect on the ground beside her.
What reason is there for her to be so wholly unafraid?
I suspect someone here is somebody else's ghost.

260

How predictable these final days of summer are!
He lies on his back in his nondescript pavilion,
Reading an uninteresting letter from a relative.
He sighs, and begins to think out a dull reply.

261

How predictable these final days of summer are!
He lies on his back in his nondescript pavilion,
Reading an uninteresting letter from a relative.
What is that strange whistling sound? It seems to be approaching.

262

How predictable these final days of summer are!
He lies on his back in his nondescript pavilion,
Reading an uninteresting letter from a relative.
The meteorite continues its beautifully timed descent.

263

The scent of normal flowers now penetrates his nostrils.
So! – he concludes – he has not been killed after all!
But the scent of exquisite music next penetrates his nostrils.
The sight of a vast lake penetrates and fills his nostrils.

264

And still the path continues climbing,
Long after the stupendous temple has been reached;
Towards an exhilarating vista, admired largely
By the irreligious, or the hopelessly unobservant.

265

The hermit cries out suddenly in understanding.
At last he has remembered who he was
In the incarnation previous to this one.
He sets out for the village, swaying his hips.

266

The morning after completing his eight million word manuscript
About the essential unreality of all things,
He searches his room in apparently increasing desperation,
Wondering where on earth it can possibly have disappeared to.

267

Waking up in one of the pavilions of heaven,
To find the earlobe of a goddess very near to his lips,
He is so disordered by the subtle sound of her breathing
That, for a joyous moment, he imagines he is still alive.

268

As he falls asleep in a pavilion of heaven,
A few blades of grass are trapped between his fingers.
One by one these subtle objects will disappear,
And he will waken up into a world he has not imagined.

269 *A Death Sentence*

'Man is no more than the briefest spark in the cycle
Of eternal change, and his life is insignificance itself
Compared with the complex universe; but, even so,
No-one farts with impunity in the Empress's presence.'

270

The dog stops suddenly in the palace gardens,
Attracted by the noise it hears in the distance.
The last time it heard a scream like that, the entire city had to be rebuilt.
Yes; there it is. The exact same pattern as before.

271

The most timorous of all the Minor Han Emperors
Cannot bear anyone approaching within forty yards of him.
All his audiences are conducted from the far end of a long hall.
Discreet ministers shout of the need for an heir, urgently.

272

The most timorous of all the Minor Han Emperors
Cannot bear anyone to approach within forty yards of him.
All his audiences are conducted from the far end of an extremely long
    hall.
Small wonder then that well-informed spies soon put an end to it all.

273

An accidental tuft of grass waves on the palace roof,
Unseen by the third Emperor, the fourth
Emperor, the fifth Emperor, the sixth
Emperor, and the seventh and last Emperor.

274

The Emperor is racing down a tunnel
Which links (or so he thinks) his private apartments
With the room of a young lady he is inordinately fond of.
Another two or three decades should see him there.

275

The cool shelter of this walled rock endures
Throughout the longest of the dynasties;
To be rested in from the heat of various noons,
Or insistent driving rainfalls which seemed, for a while, eternal.

276

The village shudders under the night rain.
The beggars huddle against the low walls.
A dog barks. The darkness grows.
A man coughs. The rain continues.

277

What should he do? Try to jump the chasm here,
Or waste hours seeking a bridge elsewhere? He jumps.
Far above, occasional passages of birdcall.
The continuing lively trickle of the stream far below.

278

The temple doors are firmly shut; the rain
Strikes the ridges and edges of the ornaments
Embossed upon them, and trickles variously
Down to the scraped feet waiting vainly outside.

279

As he walks down the road along by a high wall,
He little suspects that, on the other side,
His brother is walking through a superb garden.
Each believes the other to have died last year.

280

It is exactly this house which he has dreamed of all his life.
Exactly that scatter of mountains in the distance.
Exactly that line of trees sweeping towards him.
Exactly that neighbour's wife coughing on the balcony.

281

Daytime. The young woman is sleeping soundly.
The worrying events of the previous night are over.
A window-blind raps light against the frame.
It ceases for a while. It begins to rap again.

282

Extreme darkness – the cold tightens the water –
The occasional muffled sound from a poor row of cottages –
Probably only the action of a dream –
Utter darkness – the water ripples and breaks –

283

She clutches impulsively at the tree.
The tree scatters delirious leaves
Onto her, and onto the bureaucrat writhing beside her.
The river shouts, then instantly repents its rashness.

284

In the morning, all the Goddesses stand nobly out on their balconies.
They seem genuinely sorry that he has to leave.
Even the scented air is stuffed full of the promise of kindness.
If only he had thought in time of *pretending* to believe in them!

285

In the morning, all the Goddesses stand warmly out on their
    balconies.
They seem genuinely sorry that he has to leave.
But what else can he do? His treacherous cretinous body
Insisted on going on ahead last night, and now he has to follow it;

286

Four of the Gods are hurrying down a hillside,
Towards the mansion where the great thinker dwells
Who recently proclaimed the triunph of monotheism.
Each is secretly trying to get there before the others.

287

After lying sleepless for hours in a borrowed bed
In front of a screen depicting a roaring waterfall,
The guest begins to feel disconcertingly damp.
He turns the screen round, and lies in front of a sunrise.

288

Rain beats on the exposed hill
Above a couple of sodden, neighbourly roofs.
Under one, a husband and wife struggle.
Under the other, a husband and wife struggle.

289

An insect of enormous complexity
Walks down a plant of enormous complexity
Towards a landscape of enormous complexity
In a pot beside the head of a sleeping baby.

290

The old man puts down his wine-bowl unsteadily and gazes upwards.
A couple of geese are indeed up there, brilliantly high in the sky.
Is the flying gibbon pursuing them, or is it merely following them?
From this angle it is, as usual, difficult to be certain.

291 *Drinking Song*
'The tradition of personifying knowledge
As a young female wearing only hairpins,
A lace garter, and a small frilly collar,
Is utterly unknown here in China, unfortunately.'

292 *Drinking Song*
'. . . 195 thousand 380
Billions, 644 thousand
219 million, 507
Thousand and 41 utterly astonished corpses . . .'

293

The crowd applauds heartily at the end of the performance.
A musician picks up her zither and retires gracefully.
A musician picks up her lute and gracefully retires.
A menial steps forward, cringes, and drags away the corpses.

294

The small lake – the small bridge – the small trees –
The large flag and pennants of the rebellious general –
The moderate-sized breasts of the fleeing peasant women –
A bored God's hand closes round the globe and crushes it.

295

It would appear that Paradise is on fire;
But no-one is particularly worried by this fact.
Occasionally they turn from their wordless conversations
To smile at the flames in a profoundly understanding manner.

296

A group of tiny metal mirrors are gathered together, perhaps in a
   museum, perhaps in a small case owned by a discriminating,
   awkwardly breathing collector.
But the beautiful faces!
Sleepless nights in adjacent centuries; moments of joy separated by a
   real though legendary river.
The hands have discarded the mirrors; the faces have drifted a little
   way to right and left.

297

Being a man of almost modern sensitivity, he is bitten deeply into by
   the sight of a small hand holding the extremely delicate handle of
   the ornate jug;
But eight or ten days later – as he does not know, how should we? –
   begin the first enterprises of crushing such hands in the approaches,
   compulsions and extremes of passion;
A callousness and severity which she is resilient enough not to think it
   worth mentioning in the following morning, brushing her hair
   perhaps with hands that quite refuse to cover the amicable distances
   which her words cover;
And, five hundred years later, a little paint or enamel has been
   chipped off from the handle, but no damage more.

298

On that evening, all his former selves
Who had ever sailed over the lake, returned;
So that the empty water was instantly peopled
By men moving so often in the same direction.

299

These tiny wooden steps down the low bank,
Covered each day by different water, different mud,
From a minor tributary of the wide river
Which none of us will as much as dip a single finger into –

300

A vast pleasure garden extends down one side of the river.
There is perpetual laughter in one room or another.
And perpetually the sound of someone closing a door,
And walking quietly away off down a corridor.

Book Four

On the Eighth Floor of the Pagoda

301

A full moon on the Sung palace terraces.
Everyone of much importance is asleep.
The people walking through the corridors
Can scarcely number more than five or six hundred.

302

He is deep in meditation in his bamboo grove.
Invisible to the passers-by on the bridge.
Invisible to the passers-by on the road.
Invisible to the men in the tunnel beneath him.

303

After sitting there for an hour or so,
The poet rises, gathers up his belongings,
Gives a last glance back, and leaves the pavilion.
As soon as he leaves, another poet enters.

304

The great man, as he takes his leave of the household,
Turns for a last look at the quiet garden
Where he has spent so much time in recuperative thought.
I suppose that tree has *always* been there, has it?

305

Oh, these bridges! It is too much to believe
That each was built laboriously, with much noise –
So reassuring is the dull creak of one's footsteps,
Returning from a boring night at a retired minor official's.

306

Mist rises from the village. Noise rises from the village.
They twine together, then settle down in the night,
Like merely one more indirection in the moonlight.
The latest traveller is already coming into sight.

307

He crosses and recrosses the little bridge.
Should he go forward, or should he go back?
Was the invitation offered a serious one?
Has a happier phase of his life perhaps already begun?

308

He can hear the stream, but not see it.
Once he crosses that boundary, he is safe, surely.
Is it to the left of those trees? Is it to the right?
Freedom runs by forever just a few steps out of sight.

309

The road snakes, forgotten, through the countryside.
One more of those interminable necessary passages
Between fantastic vistas and cities we would never wish to leave.
No-one is here. So what? We are not here either.

310

Strange that the observation of running water
Should be so calming; but yes – yes – he is calm.
It has all gone wrong, and nothing matters a damn.
All those paths ahead are surely equally adequate.

311 *Drinking Song*
'Curious, the confidence with which this path leads directly to the
    edge of the precipice.
Did it once, perhaps, lead to a securer goal?
Is it fully satisfied with its present role?
If so, how few can claim as much.'

312

An empty bench faces the ocean.
Still half full of wine, a jug falls off it,
Trickles forwards, and plummets over a cliff,
Joining a hundred, two hundred ships.

313

Through the grille, waving leaves;
Not enough knowledge for so much renunciation.
Will there be a distant child crying for ever?
A little more silence; nothing more is needed.

314

He wakes up in heaven and looks around for God.
Small, timid, beating waves are the only things he sees.
What? This is just not good enough! Where are all the breasts?
He begins to suspect he has been the victim of a vicious fraud.

315

Two chambers side by side in Paradise.
Inside one, a dozen magnificent females.
Inside the other, a small fat bald man with a hammer toe.
Frankly, there are some things I just do not wish to know.

316

One must be careful where one treads in Paradise.
An infinite number of the lesser Gods
Are smaller than the least noticeable flowers;
But still they preserve a few dreadful godlike powers.

317

Last year, the form of the celebration was different.
Less emphasis was placed on the need for appeasing the gods,
And more on the sheer beauty of the peasant-girls involved.
This year, however, the emphasis is back on appeasement.

318

A naked goddess is dangling upside-down
From a roof-beam in the temple living-quarters.
This is the sort of thing she does, of course,
Only for her sincerest, most spiritual followers.

319

It is difficult not to envy the saint his serenity;
His sense of total mastery in the face
Of the elements which rage against his door,
While he sits calmly tying up a bemused whore.

320

The Goddess of Mercy lies prone in the temple garden
With a hatchet through her skull. She is not dead –
Being immortal; she is merely deep in thought.
Wasn't there some precaution this time she perhaps forgot?

321

This temple, lost among the mountains,
Is the sentry of an even higher temple
Lost even more thoroughly among the mountains.
The noonday sun is giving away as little as it can.

322
In the temple's most sacred room, he hesitates.
Can he be certain he is really alone?
He moves with irresolute steps towards the altar.
Surely now, at the moment of triumph, is not the time to falter?

323
It seems probable that someone lives in this forest.
There are so many hints available
To the trained eye. Look over there, for instance.
Or over there. Or down there. Or through there. Or in there.

324 *Drinking Song*
'After one has wandered alone down mountain paths
For eight hours, without ever meeting anybody,
One is scarcely in the ideal frame of mind
For the sight of a mystic recluse doing sad things to his behind.'

325 *Drinking Song*
'After one has wandered along severe mountain pathways
For nine hours, all without meeting anyone –
When a burly monk leaps out and tries to sell you his behind,
It does little to preserve one's transcendent frame of mind.'

326
The scholar inspects the picture behind his chair.
For the first time, he notices that the crabbed, inscribed poem
Might just be read as extolling the delights of sodomy.
Ah! Is *that* why all his friends have recently melted away?

327
No diligent judge could possibly ignore so vivid a dream.
Night after night, he has had a memorable, convincing vision,
Of a woman with the secret of the universe written on her buttocks in
    fading ink.
Let others fail to grasp where their public duty lies, if they wish.

328
Meanwhile, in another part of the same scroll,
A man who is kneeling in a forest, frantically
Hiding a severed head and a bloodied cleaver,
Is politely listening to a friend recite his poetry.

329
Not only has the poet written a poem in this album –
He has also jotted down a brief evaluation
Of the character of the man whose house he was visiting.
The rare inscription ends with a curious abruptness.

330
A doleful song comes from the small house,
Abandoned among the mountains and the clouds;
Folded safely away in nocturnal forgetfulness.
Two voices? Three voices? Impossible to tell.

331
Mist has utterly surrounded the pavilion.
Evening has deepened and almost lost itself
In the sinuosities of the steep valley.
Night should arrive soon, if it can find its way.

332
They have stayed awake throughout the entire night!
They have stayed awake, and nothing has happened to them!
Again the morning light startles the trees in the lane.
The neighbours' various voices begin to be heard again.

333 *Drinking Song*
'All day I waited for you in my small pavilion,
But no one arrived. Except for a local eccentric,
Who passed three hours of the afternoon telling me about squirrels.
You owe me several decades of your company now.'

334 *Drinking Song*
'All the fathers are at the windows, and each mother is at the gate.
The children are either coming in or leaving.
It is such a perfect morning; or it was; or it is again.
We are all born more than ten and less than fifteen seconds too late.'

335 *Drinking Song*
'This newest spring seems almost to have gone –
Ignorant of the days which I had intended
To set aside to observe it. How very like the thing!
But I shall try to love summer as if it still were spring.'

336 *Song*

'The wind stops. The bamboo returns to its calmness.
The large drab city everywhere beyond this lane
Transforms itself back into a large drab city.
Some nothing is enchanting us quite without pity.'

337

An unrestrained youth is pissing in an alleyway,
Which leads to a road, which leads to a stairway,
Where a wineshop stands, in the upper rooms of which
An old man is wondering what exactly is happening to him.

338

She gazes across the bay from inside her kitchen;
After all, one has to direct one's eyes somewhere –
Even when one is listening to absolute nonsense.
What unlikely cities are those boats vanishing to?

339

An overturned jug lies beside the wicker fence.
An overturned boat lies in the middle of the garden.
Let us hope everyone is at least still on land.
Yesterday's reunion clearly got out of hand.

340

The boat smashes against the rocks.
The boat hurtles away from the rocks.
The boat smashes against the rocks again.
I expect the fisherman is already dead.

341

Rain slides narrowly between the cottages
That fill the narrow gaps between the rocks
Which line each side of the narrow river,
Victims of a narrow, vindictive sky.

342

He sits in the garden, appearing not to notice the rain.
How long does he mean to stay there? He must be drenched by now.
I am amazed that no-one comes out to talk to him.
Not even when it at last stops, an hour or so later.

343

A God is throwing old clothes into the broad river
That stretches out inexorably down the distance,
Carrying off, to the other side of existence,
An endless cargo of damp, floating clothing.

344

Each of the fifteen mighty arches of the bridge
Represents a possible wide channel of escape
Through which the tiny toy boat may continue on its travels
Further and further away from three stepping-stones far upstream.

345

The river seems hardly in a hurry to fall.
Still it idles, although the tremendous cascade
Is by now only a second or two away –
As if endlessly seeking motives for an endless delay.

346

A tiny boat gives the lake its size.
A small sun is casting an immense light.
In spots like these, infinity is made.
It terrifies itself till it has learned its trade.

347

From here, the infinite valley stretches out ahead;
As if it extended into endless space,
Beyond the bounds of the earth. He dismounts slowly,
Fetches some food slowly, and slowly sits on the edge of the precipice.

348

When we look down from the bare ridge near the peak,
All we see is a boiling vaporous gap filled by clouds.
Yet clearly we can sense the huge lake lying beneath –
Till one of us turns round, and cries out in disbelief.

349

The beauty of this landscape is undeniable.
But not so the beauty of the intentions
Of the men on top of the seventh highest peak.
From this superb vantage-point, however, we shall hear nothing.

350

After ten hours spent among the mountains,
He passes again on his way down the same pavilion
From which he admired the view while climbing upwards earlier.
Yes, indeed. It was never lovelier than from here.

351

The old man remembers, for the first time in a year,
And looks up to the trees on the top of the mountain.
It is hard now to recall exactly which tree it was.
But his tears of joy are, all the same, horribly understandable.

352

The snow falls into the edge of the mountain.
Into a single tree, hanging out
Over an unnegotiable precipice.
And likewise into the neighbouring abyss.

353

Did he really chase a drunk, half-naked old neighbour
Through this same cold garden thirty years ago?
He leans forward to scrape at the newly fallen snow.
How can so many people manage to find gardens *innocent*?

354

They raise their voices as the servant noisily returns;
And hastily return their independent hands
To chaste apparent normality. The secluded garden
Sparkles again to a brilliant discussion of funeral urns.

355

The lady sits in the garden, surrounded by such sounds;
Smiling abstractedly, almost lost in thought.
Is this the same music, or merely similar music?
The same air? The same strain? The same time?

356

What lips will drink next from this cup,
Which a lizard crawls into and out of,
Unseen, in the abandoned garden,
Before the raindrops begin to strike it?

357
Rain is falling steadily as they enter the village.
It falls steadily as they journey through it.
It continues to fall steadily as they leave.
And it still falls steadily long after they have gone.

358
It was a perfect morning when he began his journey.
The birds carolled; the sunlight was glorious; the village
Hid its weeping girls behind calm charming walls.
But now the rain falls and falls. Not here! Where is he?

359
The branches sway and, for an instant,
The woman at the window can be seen from the road.
But no-one happens to be on the road at the moment.
Or not quite at the right point on the road.

360
The sheer mundanity of that grassy cliff above the road
Suggests that no-one has ever travelled a great distance to view it.
Yet, something about it also manages to suggest
That many have looked up at it while travelling great distances.

361
I suspect this youth here, sprinting along a windswept road,
Is also that leering elderly sage, who at present
Is talking to a weeping prostitute at a screen,
And straining to catch her reply. But I may just possibly be wrong.

362
The storm is crossing a bridge in regular pulses.
It is harrying the muddy hill in regular pulses.
It is lashing mercilessly against a wall.
It is lashing mercilessly against a wall.

363
The wind disturbs the sand a little.
The wind disturbs the sand a little more.
Is that the top of a rare box which has become visible for a moment?
The wind disturbs the sand a little more. Nothing.

364

Outside the window, the usual light.
No strange commotions in the sky this morning.
The storm has departed to wherever it is that storms depart to.
The real world, it seems, came back out of hiding during the night.

365

A bitter man hides just round a corner, listening.
The two court women he overhears are not important enough
To reveal anything worth betraying to his master –
But never has he heard of a more interesting ailment than this.

366

Four of the orchestra of court ladies,
During rehearsal, have a lengthy, foul-mouthed argument.
In his hidden gallery, the Emperor smiles hugely.
Only when the music starts up again does he leave.

367

Breaking the silence which has reigned all morning,
A group of messengers bursts out of a doorway,
Disperses and disappears through the various exits
Of the courtyard which only the Emperor should use.

368

After three days of desperate riding,
The ambassador is at last intercepted
Before he can deliver his inflammatory message.
He is handed an *even more* inflammatory message.

369

Only to the 98th urgent message
Does a reply finally come, curtly, from the delayed ambassador
Who had been sent down to that notoriously dissolute court,
And ordered to return, asap, with a full report.

370

The four girls giggling in the remote palace room,
Trying on one ridiculous garment after another,
Are surprised when, after an hour, a cupboard quickly opens,
And a venerable ambassador hurries out past them, weeping.

371

Midnight in the outer rooms of the palace.
Cautiously a figure emerges from a box.
It strides over and inspects the various locks;
Then sighs, and returns quickly to its hiding-place.

372

For two consecutive days the fire rages;
Devouring the palace in successive stages.
Stairway after stairway crumbles and falls.
Corpses tumble out from behind collapsing walls.

373

Door after door at the front of the palace lies open,
And it is far from clear which are guarded and which are not.
Will it be safe to try to get in through this one here?
After all, he has not been unexpected there for over a year.

374

An incessant hammering on the door
Announces the arrival of late April.
He wakens up from a confused dream of trees,
And tries to right himself on oddly disobedient knees.

375

The man slumped, dreaming, in the small pavilion
Is the same man as the one climbing the mountain path towards him.
The sleeping figure snorts, changing the position of a leg
The other stumbles and nearly falls – but recovers himself just in
    time.

376 *Drinking Song*

'A man is climbing up the outside of the city wall.
An hour of exertion has taken him only halfway there.
It would be most unlikely for him to survive a fall.
I do really feel rather bad about throwing these stones at him.'

377

Some Gods are playing at the top of a very thin mountain.
They hide behind trees, and sometimes try to touch each other.
Occasionally one will slip, and, after falling
For an hour or so, will stop, and begin to reascend.

378

A goddess lies, almost trapped by some fallen branches.
She watches as a passing monk, overcome by passion,
Begins to investigate her in an acutely personal fashion.
Well, one has to allow one's followers *some* leeway, I suppose.

379

A wet leaf clinging to a threshold
Gradually dries, crispens, and falls to the ground,
There to join an enormous heap of other leaves.
A royal dog wanders up to the heap and pisses on it.

380

Nervously, he lifts the elixir to his lips.
Among its ingredients are at least five poisons.
Perhaps he should let the dog taste it first?
But could the country tolerate an immortal dog?

381

The swan sails serenely past that point on the riverbank
Where the greatest poet of the last six hundred years
Is running about in something approaching ecstasy.
Elegantly, it reappears in a letter of the next century.

382

I shall leave after the tenth boat passes this point,
Thinks the old traveller, resting on the riverbank.
But when the tenth boat passes, an hour or so later,
He is already lying prone in a town lane.

383

The 97 year-old poet staggers and falls.
Such a brilliant utterance came into his mind just then
That the glory overstrained his heart. Inch by inch, he crawls
Towards his writing-bench. How cruelly distant it is.

384

Arriving hurriedly at an august friend's house,
With a scroll from a great new poet he has just discovered,
He sees a couple of women carrying him in through his gate.
Ah well. Perhaps tomorrow. Literature can always wait.

385

Meanwhile, in another part of the same scroll,
The woman who was lying on the floor, smiling,
Is walking up a hidden stairway, smiling
A subtler variation of the same smile.

386

Two ladies stand in a garden, smiling distantly.
How distantly? 7 provinces, 13 big rivers,
12,362 walls, and two buildings
In which great writers are at work. And now they've both gone out
    anyway.

387

Ah! That's a nice place! I would like to live there,
Thinks the monk, caught by a sudden view of a house
Nestling on the hillside. And, the next morning,
He does indeed wake up inside it, smiling contentedly.

388

They call out to each other across the wide river.
Neither quite understands what the other one is saying;
But each resettles the old woman upon his shoulders,
And continues on into the forest, smiling.

389

The light streaming out from the small house,
From a modest lamp standing beside the window,
Manages to thread its way deep into the forest,
Thanks to the complicity of innumerable trees.

390

A boy among flowers, the cats watching him move.
A boy among cats, the flowers waving beside them.
Is the mother smiling at this from a window not far away;
Or is the window where she might be at the moment unoccupied?

391

The surprised forger sighs, politely apologizes,
And neatly jumps sideways out of the window of the brothel.
The owner's nephew, barely restraining his tears,
Clambers back laboriously into his female attire.

392

The suspicious husband knocks over the screen.
He gasps in surprise. As does his audience.
For the lustful tea merchant, who should stand smirking there,
Is seated, pinned by some arrows to a cheap chair.

393

The crane strides resolutely into the room,
Searches for it in one place after another,
Finds it beneath the bed, grasps it in its claws,
And exits through the door to tumultuous applause.

394

The bird which lands for a moment beside
The great artist, does not at first realise
Its new neighbour is not merely more foliage,
Or sense that for over a minute it is being watched.

395

The artist closes his door behind him, and turns
Towards an uncompleted painting of a valley.
Look! Someone has slipped in and finished it off!
The drowsing black-and-white cat emits a modest cough.

396

This bizarre artist paints by dipping his penis in ink.
The effects are more successful than you might anticipate.
Even so, his landscapes are probably finer than his portraits.
But his religious pictures are quite extraordinarily convincing.

397

Page after page the sage covers in his wonderful flowing script,
Describing how the innermost principles of the universe cannot
    possibly be described.
Impossibility after impossibility is brilliantly pinpointed.
Very near the thousandth page, he screams and tears the whole thing up.

398

The curiously realistic scroll picture of a desert
Begins to seep sand down onto the sleeping figure
Slumped over a desk beneath it, writing-brush in hand.
The level rises higher and higher beyond his ankles.

399

Rocks begin to fall out of the dreaming scholar's head.
A tree or two. A small stream.
Soon the room where he lies has become a charming landscape.
A party of drunks arrive, and sit down, laughing.

400

Landscape after landscape is stored inside the cupboard.
The owner has travelled to the eastern capital
To argue his right to demolish a neighbour's wall.
Twenty endless valleys sleep in a set of boxes.

Book Five

Many Expected Travellers

401

Carrying his newly completed map of an old capital
Through the warren of tiny lanes behind the new palace,
The great cartographer has unfortunately got lost.
He screws up his courage, and taps at one of the doors.

402

The landscape, perfectly preserved for centuries,
Passed down carefully from descendant to descendant,
Though frequently unlooked at for an entire decade,
Is carried secretly through a wall at dead of night.

403

Inordinately proud of his superb whiskers,
The officer strides down the lane,
Rereading a passionate letter of assignation
Recently found in a clump of vegetation.

404

Reaching right down, he discovers a hidden letter, left
By the wife of his previous neighbour forty years before.
He screens his eyes, and tries to remember her face.
Such passion in such an unremembered place!

405

He lies dreaming in a small house, in a rugged landscape.
He is either 14 years old, or 73.
A light wind plays with the leaves on the nearest lawn.
He stretches on his wide couch in the imminent dawn.

406

The bemused sage is in something of a quandary.
After insisting for so many years that truth lies beyond utterance,
He has just dreamed fifty words that say almost everything.
This is clearly going to be one of those *difficult* days.

407

The vast temple ceremonial hall is an abandoned ruin.
The words of immense wisdom have long since been spoken;
Have teased the air on each day of adjoined centuries;
And have disappeared well beyond this light, perfect breeze.

408

Two lords and five ladies are walking up a mountain path
Towards a temple, to expiate an impiety.
Every so often, one of them begins to giggle.
Oh – this is rather alarming. Now two of them are giggling.

409

Three men are sleeping on the bank of a river.
One is dreaming of his wife as she was ten years before.
One is dreaming of a woman putting on her ear ornaments.
One is dreaming of a woman taking off her ear ornaments.

410

At which point the Censor screamed and said, 'Enough!'
One of the women instantly let go of his ears.
Another instantly began to pull out all the needles.
And a third of them stopped covering a fourth in fluff.

411

The emperor gives a signal, and the contest begins.
Instantly, the five monks on the terraces
Start trying to be aware of the deepest secrets of the universe.
It should certainly be most instructive to see who wins.

412

The two rivals bow to each other in a clearing.
They take six steps backwards, remove their cloaks,
Reach down to grapple with two very large rocks,
And stagger fiercely towards each other, carrying them.

413

In the mist, the rocks seem almost to be imbued with life –
Bringing vividly to mind that old legend of the prince
Who fell in love with a well-shaped rock, kissed a tiny dent on its
    surface,
And died of fright when it turned into his dead wife.

414

Why does this garden rock so remind him of his late wife?
Each morning he goes out to sit beside it –
Until, one glorious forenoon, it collapses on top of him.
His cries of delirious happiness slowly become weaker and weaker.

415 *Drinking Song*
'A handful of rocks and trees fill the walled garden.
Twenty paces give one twenty views.
Which view is the old scholar admiring at the moment?
Or rather: which *shall* he admire when the singing-girl has climbed
     back up off his neck?'

416
Yesterday, drunk, he wagered on a single throw of the dice
His fine town house against a look at his friend's wife's sister's backside.
Now he wanders through the garden, taking a last farewell.
It was lovely here, of course; still, a house is only a house.

417
The scholar strikes his forehead in horror.
Has he forgotten to bring the wine with him again?
But, no. It is the classic texts he has forgotten.
Ah, well. One can't be expected to remember everything.

418
By a tree at the edge of the river, two distinguished scholars
Are discussing an important topic in cultured, profound voices –
Disdaining to notice the passing bargee who hollers,
'My wife will do anything for a hundred dollars!'

419
Oh God, no! No! The Imperial Barge is sinking!
And with it go, surely to be irrecoverably lost,
All 187 volumes of the Recent Official State History.
Oh, why did the would-be salvagers have to turn up so late?

420
The colourful tough thorny plant
Forces its way through the paving-stones
Of the long since abandoned capital
And waves anyway, slightly outside history.

421
The abandoned palace is overrun by trees;
Numerous, almost, as the courtiers who once drifted there.
The fallen leaves are as plentiful as past compliments.
Poisonous snakes glide among the fallen leaves.

422

He shelters against a wall at the height of the storm;
Watching the debris being blown past him.
Twigs, branches, leaves, tiles, occasional items of clothing;
And a strikingly original collection of pauses.

423

Every third minute of the morning, a different pregnant woman
Is ushered into the presence of the motionless Emperor;
Where she strips off and pauses, till the Chamberlain finds out
If *she* has stopped him brooding over this latest rout.

424

Quietly, the Governor raises his head
From the desk on which he has lain it in despair.
He listens to the sounds of the fighting, still distant;
Then sinks his head slowly back down onto the table.

425

The soldier lies beside the rock, almost frozen to death.
Only an occasional puff of exhaled, frozen breath.
Did the siege fail? Did the siege succeed?
Where does that ditch run to? Over there. What?

426

The soldier pulls his coat even more tightly about himself.
How cold it is at this benighted posting.
Who is it China is being protected from this time?
Ah, well. It should be dawn in less than an hour anyway.

427

The dog gazes fixedly at an approaching figure.
Never before has he seen such bizarre clothing.
Could this be one of those ridiculous foreigners
Whose cowardice used to delight his now strangely vanished master?

428

The servant-girl starts to offer an explanation –
But the master's outstretched hand cuts her off dead.
She must be punished, as per regulation.
She sighs, then stands submissively on her head.

429

Having been kept waiting for almost a full hour,
The prince frowns as the Zen Master bounds out into the garden,
Wiggling his exposed penis, and shouting, 'I'm a bit of a lad!'
This had better presage a very great truth indeed.

430 *Drinking Song*

'I have lately been petitioning the Emperor
To have my father's penis declared a zone
Of overwhelming historical interest –
But he keeps fobbing me off with limp excuses.'

431 *Drinking Song*

'My penis is 37 *jia* long! Yes!
My manly appendage is 103 *tsan* long! Yes! Yes!
My most vital piece of natural equipment is 672 *chang* long! Yes! Yes! Yes!
I would rather not swing through the trees just at the moment, if you
     don't mind.'

432 *Drinking Song*

'One morning, we shall waken, and everything will be laughter.
We will see everything without self-delusion.
Yes; even our genitalia shall seem inevitable.
Tomorrow? Perhaps. But much more probably the day after.'

433

Three Gods are standing by the side of the road,
Laughing uproariously at some labouring peasants.
Of course, the peasants are unable to see them;
But they *can* hear the spiritual laughter, which is surely a little off-putting.

434

One of the people in this room is divine.
The scholars laughing at her pronunciation
Do not yet realise it; though there is a frown
On the face of the one who so lately glanced inside her gown.

435

She plucks a blossom and puts it into her hair.
A briar deftly reaches out and pulls off her gown.
One ought to be more careful in a magician's garden.
He chuckles happily in his hidden, silent lair.

436

The breeze drifts through their now neglected lute-strings.
No-one will disturb them here for the whole day.
Ah, how pleasant to be released from the restrictions of office;
And to sit, drunk, in a garden, doing two or three very wrong things!

437

The door closes behind them yet again,
And they retire once more into their private realm.
A subtle tactful breeze dislocates leaves on an elm.
The quiet passageway shivers now and then.

438

During his walk he has crossed perhaps nine or ten bridges.
This is not particularly unusual in such a town.
Now, if one had collapsed – that *would* have been unusual.
He closes his door and disappears from sight.

439

It is once again a clear morning in the valley.
Possibly it has rained during the night.
A man crawls laboriously through his front door, at last;
Closes it behind him, and collapses, unconscious.

440

Only a few rocks separate the two riverside dwellings.
The figure who crawls laboriously out of one,
Making tortured progress back to the other,
Is neatly covered by livid, perplexing swellings.

441

So peculiar, these rocks and tight clumps of tree.
A dozen large rocks, with pathways between them.
So many different continents to inhabit;
And never out of hearing of the same trivial river.

442

A small bridge – suddenly there among the steep, grooved hills.
So, I am expected to take this path after all –
And its diffident progress is not my own discovery.
I feel as if half of history is hiding nearby, watching me.

443 *Drinking Song*

'This path through the wood keeps turning left and right,
Like someone unable to make up his mind.
Whereas I am merely unable to make up my mind
Whether or not to abandon progress for the night.'

444

The man about to cross the bridge has obviously regained his
    memory.
He looks over to the path on the other side of the lake.
Is the house still there? There should be a house there.
To his surprise, he can count 37 houses there.

445

There are always small neat houses across the river.
There are always people moving far in the distance.
Always a feeling of a horizon of reasonably sized towns
Amicably changing and exchanging their casual visitors.

446

They sit on a finger of land, awaiting the return of the ferry.
To while away the time, they tell each other stories
Of river beasts and unfortunate travellers.
When the ferry returns, no-one is waiting for it.

447

When he reaches the small hilltop, he finds to his surprise
That there is in fact nobody there after all.
But surely he glimpsed somebody up there, during his climb?
Nor is the view even particularly sublime.

448

Beyond the preliminary peaks lies a great wall of snow
That curves off into the empty air at such height.
Dynasties pass, and no human footsteps appear on it.
Yet, every year, some footsteps appear on it.

449

A full moon above the snowy peaks.
Dark, but everything is touched by brightness.
Late, but another world seems about to start,
In which there will never again be any mention of sunlight.

450

A full moon above the snowy peaks.
Dark, but everything is touched by brightness.
Late, but the universe seems about to start,
Once the last few finishing touches have quite been perfected.

451

The gate is open although it is late at night.
The bright moon throws shadows into the quiet yard.
A few of the shadows drift around as the wind blows.
But most soon move back to their original positions.

452

Why is the philosopher no longer sitting on that knoll?
Has he fallen over the edge? Has he gone back home?
The moon is now high above the distant forest.
It is almost certain he has gone back home.

453

The moon rises again on the day after
The collapse of the precarious pavilion.
And, for the first night of 50,000,
A now forgotten grave is directly touched by moonlight.

454

The old sage has surpassed himself on his walk.
In triumph, having travelled higher than ever before,
He is about to stride across a remote bridge
Which has been waiting to collapse for a quarter century.

455

Two men are standing on a bridge, looking at the moon.
They hear a distant carriage. They do not move
Off the exposed bridge, to a safer position.
The distant carriage somewhere returns to the distance.

456

Two men are standing on a bridge, looking at the moon.
Far away, the sound of a single horse.
There is a place on earth for it to go to too.
Two men beside each other, both looking at the moon.

457 *An Inscription*
I stop the carriage within view of the hill-gardens.
The horses fret and stamp, as if ill at ease.
How often it had been our intention to come here again.
The carriage still has sufficient space for us both.

458
A woman is kneeling in front of a garden shrine,
Praying for her husband's safe return.
Inside her body, her child moves for the first time.
Her husband drinks morosely on a remote grime-blown road.

459 *Drinking Song*
'Someone has written something on the mountain shrine.
Some previous visitor has scribbled an inscription,
Describing a recent crudely sexual experience.
Why does it sound more lively than any of mine have ever done?'

460
Icicles rattle on the lower branches of the tree.
Perhaps an intruder has brushed against them.
Perhaps an intruder has not brushed against them.
Someone is noisily drinking his first tea of the morning.

461
What thought-provoking sounds issue from the sage's study.
Those mellifluous runs, elegantly drawn from a long-necked lute.
That gasp of surprise, and brief noise of tearing fabric.
That door slamming; that outburst of mature, wise tears.

462
Ah! What heart-warming sounds issue from the sage's study.
He is, as usual, teaching one of the servant-girls to read.
Listen to that soft, low voice, stammering through something of
    Confucius;
Trembling with a passion one rarely associates with Confucius.

463
After reading through 90 canonical texts about purity,
The sage sighs with relief; stands up; puts
A melon under each armpit; looks round;
And hurries off to a place of greater privacy.

464

The newly wed wife, quaking elegantly on the bed,
Watches in stark silence as her muscular husband returns
And deposits a thousand bananas onto the pillow beside her.
Only now does she recall what her weeping mother-in-law once said.

465

As a highlight of the lordly marriage celebrations,
The very famous dancer performs his very famous sword dance –
Using five blades for the first time instead of his normal four.
That evening, much of the food remains uneaten.

466

Listening to the eery echoing of his footsteps,
As he proceeds further and further into the imperial hall,
He becomes so nervous that he lets the dagger drop from his sleeve.
Nervously, he asks the new king for permission to leave.

467

Trees – trees – a breath from the mountains
Blowing through the open door – the old man
Lifts his head weakly from the floor, expecting
A visitor – but the visitor is not yet here.

468

When he reaches the small hilltop, he finds to his surprise
That there is in fact nobody there after all.
There is no-one there at all; not even himself.
He can hardly believe the non-evidence of his own eyes.

469

Today there vas no-one sitting on the treestump.
Nor was there anyone sitting there yesterday.
Nor will there be anyone sitting there tomorrow.
The last such uneventful sequence was over three centuries ago.

470

In exaltation, he reaches the edge of the sea,
And continues walking. For the first century
All goes well. The second century
Is also, broadly, passable. But the third century . . .

471
Today there was no-one sitting on the treestump.
Nor was there anyone sitting there yesterday.
Nor shall there be anyone sitting there tomorrow.
The next such uneventful sequence will happen eight centuries later.

472
The picture is so old that it has almost entirely faded away.
Only the suggestion of a high wall and a few trees –
Below something which may be an astonishingly lofty mountain;
Or the stain caused by a winebowl knocked over centuries ago.

473
Sunset – sunset – sunset – sunset –
Hill after hill turns golden, and then cools.
A ripple of such cherishable moments
Runs like a quiet wave down the chain of ridges.

474
After this last ridge, there is a valley of days in length;
Where two armies could pass each other unnoticed.
Are two armies, in fact, passing each other unnoticed?
I doubt it; but let us stay and watch for a little longer anyway.

475
As the traveller passes window after window,
He sees women sitting behind window after window;
As if some dazzling procession had just run by
Which not all of his haste can quite make him catch up with.

476
Outside, a fresh bright wind rustles the golden bamboo;
Where the sage, almost weeping, in his calm chaste retreat
Is gazing for hour after hour at the large exposed feet
Of a friendless female traveller who he hopes is only sleeping.

477
A pleasant afternoon on this empty road.
The occasional flurried shower, but nothing more
Disturbs the serenity. Then all is as before.
The tired genius on the verandah continues to snore.

478
Two men are standing on a high bridge.
Above them, a long expanse of empty air.
Then another high bridge – this time unoccupied.
I suspect someone was there on it a few seconds ago.

479
The man walking along a thin rope bridge
Connecting two spots on barely accessible crags
Is wearing a pair of antlers like a stag's.
He passes on, smiling, and quietly rounds a corner.

480
Mist rises from the village. Noise rises from the village.
They twine together, then settle down in the night,
Like merely one more indirection in the moonlight.
The latest traveller is already just out of sight.

481
Trees – trees – a breath from the mountains
Blowing through the open door – the old man
Lifts his head weakly from the floor, expecting
A visitor – but the visitor has long since gone.

482
Autumn. The old feeling of sadness
Assaults one as one turns the corner
Of the pathway above the town, to discover
That absolutely everyone seems to agree it is evening again.

483
All day the column of troops has filed into the capital city;
Suggesting somewhere a group of vast squares slowly filling;
Departing from an emptiness in the hearts
Of a vast, never gathered column of women.

484
Offhandedly scanning the latest census figures,
Which report 159,000 horses in the summer capital,
The palace official walks down a quiet corridor
To the empty office of his superior.

485

The court lady's eyes grow large with gratitude
When the Empress's Assistant Official Flatterer,
Happening to meet her in a corridor,
Decides to practise on her eyebrows for a few seconds.

486

The scout left 147 soldiers behind him in this steep-walled plain.
Yet, when he returned, he found nothing but water-buffaloes there.
Cautiously, he begins to count the water-buffaloes.
He shakes his head, looks round, and begins to count again.

487

A precise miniature avalanche of four large boulders
Accounts for him as he crosses the mountain path.
For him; for his dog; for his buffalo; and for his local guide.
But not, curiously enough, for his deeply unhappy bride.

488

Now there is only a single point in the distance
To indicate the recently departed over-zealous tax-gatherer.
And now five other dots suddenly join him in the distance.
Well, so much for the recently departed tax-gatherer.

489

Two scholarly friends in a boat with a servant-girl
Are somewhat surprised when the local river-god looms up
And demands a human sacrifice right there and then.
A desperate fight breaks out between the two men.

490

The two elegant retired scholars notice with much displeasure
The arrival of a boorish comrade on the path below.
They disappear into the bamboo thickets in silent unison.
A few embarrassed colleagues, they find, are already there.

491

The reeds and flowers at the water's edge
Seem to have grown totally disproportionate
To the narrow stream which is almost lost amidst them.
Or so I thought for the almost full day I lay there.

492

This is absurd. Another fork in the road!
Already I have had to make three clear guesses –
And am quite possibly irredeemably lost.
Or, can the last frontier already have been crossed?

493

Day after day, he has taken that memory
Of a girl's happy face, seen in an eating-house,
Deeper and deeper and deeper into this out-of-the-way province.
He reaches a door; stops at it; laughs; and turns back.

494

The Western Liang dialect for 'Will you give yourself to me?'
Is strikingly similar to the Eastern Liang phrase
For, 'Which of these dusty roads, madam, will lead me to the coast?'
Many expected travellers never reach the coast.

495

Eventually the dust drifts quietly back down
And settles for a while on the last remaining courtyard
In the shape of that very rare but so treasurable character
For 'the deep peace of ultimate defeat'.

496 *Drinking Song*

'Am I really in the courtyard of the pagoda?
Am I really on the fifth floor of the pagoda?
Am I really on the eighth floor of the pagoda?
But surely this pagoda has only seven floors in all?'

497 *Drinking Song. Perpetuum Mobile.*

'If this world is an illusion, then our belief
That this world is an illusion, is also an illusion.
As, of course, must be the belief, that *if*
This world is an illusion, then our belief . . .' (etcetera)

498

Somewhere in this house there must be an instrument
That will allow him to preserve this morning unchanged for ever.
Into room after room he goes, searching;
Out of room after room he comes, content.

499

Another pleasant day to walk down the hilly lane.
And perhaps hear women talking in some of the houses
Which the warm sun reflects from – or perhaps not.
In which case, a pleasant day to walk down the hill in silence.

500

Another enchanting avenue lies open in front of him.
Is it an hour ago that he was expected in the palace?
He has spent more time in thought than he had intended to.
Perhaps it would be better not to go there at all today.

501

Slowly dust floats down, onto the palace lakes.
Charred spars sink deeper into the lush turf.
Through the wide corridors runs an occasional surf.
Clearly, one of the final dynasty's final mistakes.